DUCKS

Jill Bailey

Illustrated by
Jackie Harland

Language Consultant:
Diana Bentley
University of Reading

PUFFIN BOOKS

Notes for parents and teachers
Each title in this series has been specially written and
designed as a first natural history book for young readers.
For less able readers there are introductory captions,
while the more detailed text explains each illustration.

Contents

All the words that are
in **bold** are explained in
the glossary on page 31.

Ducks are birds.

Ducks are birds that spend most of the time swimming. They have heavy bodies and very short legs, so they waddle as they walk, but they move easily in water. Ducks have wide, flat beaks and long necks. Look at these ducks. They are called mallards.

Ducks live near water.

Ducks live in large **flocks** for most of the year. They are found in ponds, lakes, rivers and sometimes in the sea. They are very good at swimming and diving. They use their **webbed feet** as paddles when they swim. Their feathers have a waterproof coating of oil. Air trapped under the feathers helps ducks to float.

Ducks feed on tiny water animals and plants.

Ducks use their wide beaks to sift seeds, bits of pondweed, tiny water insects and shellfish from the water. They can even turn upside down to look for food under water. This is called **dabbling**. When they have finished feeding, they shake the water off their feathers before swimming away.

The male duck has colourful feathers.

Most of the year the male duck, who is called the **drake**, is much more colourful than the female. He has a bright yellow beak, but in the autumn he changes his coat and becomes brown like the female. She is called the **duck** and she has dull brown feathers with a small bright blue patch on each wing. A duck's beak is greenish-brown.

In spring the female duck chooses a male.

In early spring the drakes look for ducks to **mate** with. They raise their bright green head feathers, and tilt up their tails to show off their black, curly tail feathers. Sometimes they pretend to drink, flipping their beaks in and out of the water, or they throw their heads back over their shoulders as if they are **preening**. This is called **displaying** and a duck will swim after the drake she chooses, nodding her head at him.

13

The male duck mates with the female.

So that the duck can produce eggs, the drake must put a special liquid inside the female, called **sperm**. This happens during mating. Now the eggs can start to grow inside the duck's body. Once the eggs are laid, the drake leaves the duck. He does not stay to watch his family grow up.

The mother duck makes a nest for her eggs.

The duck makes a nest under a bush or up in a tree. She scrapes a hollow and lines it with special soft feathers called **down**. She plucks the down from her own breast. Then she lays her eggs in the nest. The eggs are pushed out of her body through a small opening just in front of her tail.

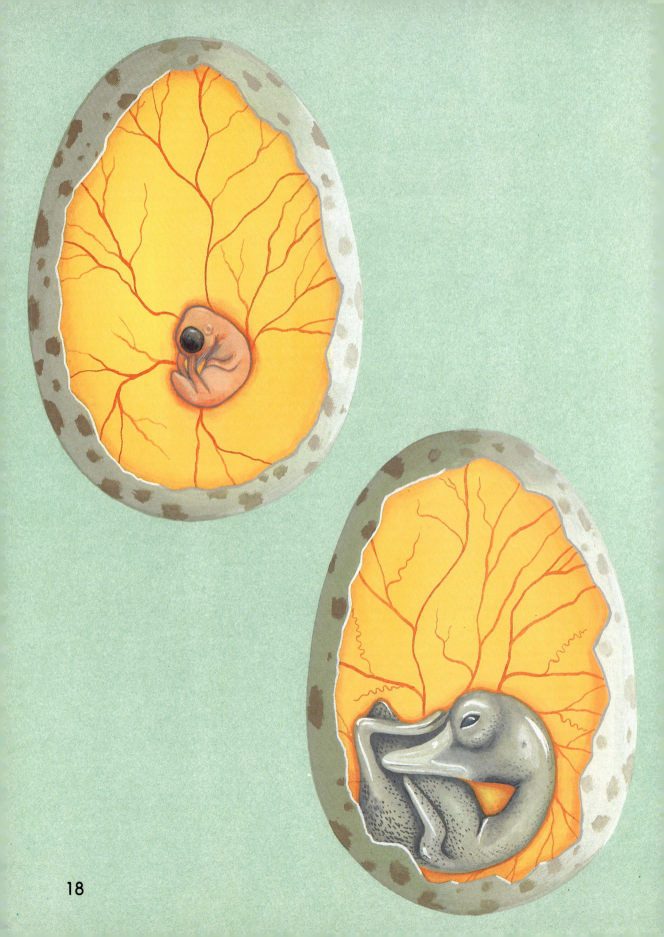

18

The baby ducks grow inside the eggs.

Inside each growing egg is a tiny duck. It is attached to a bag of thick yellow liquid called **yolk**. The yolk is a special food for the growing baby. The rest of the egg is filled with a clear liquid. As each egg passes through the duck's body on its way to be laid, a hard shell forms around it.

The mother duck sits on her eggs to keep them warm.

A mother duck can lay about thirteen greenish-grey eggs. She sits on the eggs to keep them warm. This helps the baby ducks inside to grow faster. If the mother duck leaves the nest, she covers the eggs with down and leaves. This keeps them warm and helps to hide them from enemies.

The baby ducks **hatch** out of their eggs.

After twenty-eight days, the eggs hatch. The baby **ducklings** peck their way out using a special **egg tooth** on the tips of their beaks. The egg tooth will fall off later. The ducklings have soft, fluffy black and yellow feathers, but they are not yet waterproof. Within a few hours they can run around and feed themselves.

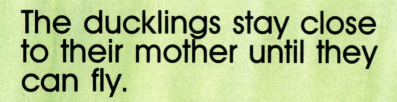

The ducklings stay close to their mother until they can fly.

After two days the ducklings' feathers are waterproof, and their mother leads them to the water. The mother duck stays with them to keep them warm and protect them from danger.

Ducks have many enemies. Foxes, stoats, cats, hawks, eagles and even some very large fish like to eat them.

The young ducks leave their mother to start their own families.

The ducklings can swim without having to take lessons. But they cannot fly until their wings have grown bigger. This takes about two months. Then they leave their mother. Next spring they will choose their own drakes or display to attract a duck. What do you think will happen then?

Feeding and watching ducks.

In most parks there is a pond where ducks live. If there is a park near you take some stale bread, broken into small pieces, and throw it into the pond. If you throw the bread close to the side of the pond, the ducks will come to the edge to feed and you can have a good look at them.

Remember to visit the ducks in early spring, so that you can see the drakes displaying to the ducks. Then, after four or five weeks, you will see the newly-hatched ducklings. Always ask an adult to take you to the park and be very careful not to go too near the water.

The life cycle of a duck.

How many stages of the life cycle of a duck can you remember?

Glossary

Dabbling When ducks feed upside down in the water, this is called dabbling.

Displaying This is when drakes show off to attract female ducks.

Down Very soft feathers from the mother's breast, which she uses to line her nest.

Drake A male duck.

Duck A female duck.

Ducklings Baby ducks.

Egg tooth A special tooth on the tip of the beak which the duckling uses to peck its way out of the egg. The egg tooth falls off soon after hatching.

Flocks Groups of birds.

Hatch To break out of an egg.

Mate This is when male (father) and female (mother) animals join together. It is how a baby animal is made.

Preening When a bird smears its feathers with oil, this is called preening. The oil comes from a special patch just below the tail.

Sperm A liquid from the male duck which mixes with the eggs inside the female's body. If this does not happen, the eggs will not grow.

Webbed feet Feet whose toes are joined by flaps of skin.

Yolk A special liquid which provides food for the baby duck inside each egg.

Finding out more

Here are some books to read to find
out more about ducks.

Birth of a Duckling by H-H. Isenbart (J.M. Dent, 1980)
Discovering Ducks, Geese and Swans by A. Wharton
    (Wayland, 1987)
Ducks and Ducklings by T. Udagawa (Wayland, 1980)
Egg to Chick by M.E. Selsam (Windmill Press, 1972)

Index